# LET ME BE ALONE:

## Having a serious,trusting relationship allows us to truly be our true selves.

**Eileen Vandervort**

# TABLE OF CONTENT

# **<u>INTRODUCTION</u>**

As we get older, there is a lot of pressure on us to "make it," especially in this day and age of social media.

Often, it seems like pushing through life alone is the best way to accomplish it. It is, after all, your adventure. Who better to rely on than yourself? Taking other people into account might sometimes undermine your ambitions. When you've already committed to your calling, it's difficult to commit to relationships.

Having a relationship, though, does not imply committing your whole life to them. You may still be self-sufficient while having someone by your side while you seek and accomplish your objectives.

Because there are certain things you can't do alone, and getting through life is one of them.

# Chapter 1

# **<u>Why we all need a partner</u>**

Relationships are important for a variety of reasons, including increased emotional well-being; stability; learning how to be a good friend or mate; having someone to count on and trust in times of need; someone to vent to when we face challenges; and friends and mates remove loneliness and make us feel included. Each of our interactions elicits unique emotions in us, allowing us to develop and learn about ourselves. Relationships are often the glue that binds us together amid hard events and life challenges. We would have a deadened spirit and a lack of connection to our genuine selves if we did not have interaction!

Men and women need various types of partnerships for different reasons. We tend to draw toward those who are similar to us since we have similar occupations, locations we visit, and interesting activities and interests. Therefore, connections are essential in order to have people that make us better. However, men and women have different ways of forming long-lasting ties with others. Women are far more emotionally attached and dependent on girlfriends or partners for things like parenting counsel, romantic pleasure, someone to assist with their children's growth and cognitive capacities, and learning how to be better at life and in a relationship and learn from experiences. Men do not have to be emotionally connected to experience sexual pleasure from other women, but proximity is important to them just as much as it is to women. When men participate in activities like going to the gym or watching athletic events together, they are not nearly as emotionally committed. In reality, most guys arrive, do the agreed action, and then depart without ever considering what went wrong, whether there were muddled words, or if the other person is okay. Men are better at compartmentalizing their emotions in relationships, but women tend to carry grudges, take longer to cope with emotional baggage, and let conflicts persist. Men progress more quickly in relationships, making it simpler for them to connect with people of the opposite sex and those of the same sex. Relationships are often mirrors that show us what we need to alter in order to be better partners and friends. Also, our friends and long-term connections enable us to be vulnerable and seek support in ways we wouldn't with total strangers. When we are in partnerships, we often meet new individuals through the ones we already know and expand our networks! It's exciting to have diverse life experiences, to genuinely realize who you are, to teach them intriguing new things, and to go on new adventures together.

Relationships teach us how to love and be loved, as well as who we want to be and who we don't want to be in life. Having meaningful, trustworthy connections helps us to be our authentic selves. We must be open to meeting new people, and establishing spiritual relationships will help us strengthen our faith and encourage others to do the same. Simply being yourself will attract the right people into your life for the right reasons. Always be yourself, and others will appreciate it!

## Some of the benefit of having a partner:

## You are inspired by your life partner.

Nobody delivers advice like them. This kind of life mate is someone you admire. They listen to you without passing judgment and assist you in getting to know yourself better.

They understand how to challenge you so that you may push yourself to be better in school, career, relationships, and life.

## A life mate is there for you.

It is said that blood is thicker than water.

The term "family" may refer to both relatives and individuals you've grown to consider family. This family gives the type of support that only comes from really knowing someone.

Nothing in life is ever certain, yet their dependability makes them one of your constants.

## A life partner has faith in you.

Friends come and go—that's the unfortunate fact of growing up.However, not this one. This is a relationship that spans time and space. They're your go-to when you have good or terrible news. Every second you spend in their company is enjoyable, whether it's a brief coffee date or a vacation out of the country.

You know you've got a life partner in them even while you're both out doing your own thing in the adulting cosmos.

**A life companion brightens one's life.**

Finding a love companion is a time-consuming procedure that most individuals would rather avoid.

If you discover "the one," you'll have someone to be with through good and terrible times. Living with someone on a daily basis may not always be simple, but compassion, loyalty, and compromise all contribute to a pleasant, long-lasting relationship.

## Security

Having someone to look after you financially, in case anything goes wrong with your health, or just to cuddle with you after a hard day makes you feel secure.

A life companion is fantastic if you flourish knowing you have someone to call.

## Trust

Being single is good, but without genuinely knowing someone, trust cannot exist. It is all about sharing your life with someone and believing that they would come home to you, embrace you, confide in you, and listen to you.

## Intimacy

The intimacy of having a life partner is unparalleled. Committing oneself to someone for life creates a closeness that a fling cannot provide. It's not about sex, passion, or time constraints. It is beyond words.

# Chapter 2

## <u>How to build good relationship with your partner</u>

Every relationship is unique, and individuals come together for many different reasons. Part of what constitutes a good relationship is having a clear aim for precisely what you want the relationship to be and where you want it to go. And that's something you'll only know through discussing it truly and honestly with your partner.However, there are also several features that most good partnerships have in common. Whatever your goals or challenges are, knowing these fundamental concepts will help keep your relationship engaging, rewarding, and exciting.

- **Spend quality time together.**

You fall in love while staring at each other and listening to each other. You may prolong the falling in love experience throughout time if you continue to look and listen in the same attentive manner. You undoubtedly remember when you were initially dating your significant other. Everything felt new and wonderful, and you probably spent hours conversing or brainstorming new, interesting things to try. However, as time passes, the pressures of work, family, other commitments, and the desire we all have for alone time may make it more difficult to spend time together.

Face-to-face interaction in early dating days is increasingly supplanted by rushed texts, emails, and instant messaging for many couples. While digital communication is useful for certain things, it does not have the same good influence on your brain and nervous system as face-to-face conversation. Sending a text or voice message to your partner that says "I love you" is wonderful, but if you seldom look at them or have the opportunity to sit down with them, they will believe you don't understand or respect them. And as a pair, you'll grow more estranged or distant. The emotional signals you both need to feel loved can only be delivered in person, so make time for each other no matter how hectic life becomes.

Make a commitment to spending quality time together on a regular basis. Take a few minutes each day, no matter how busy you are, to put away your technological gadgets, stop thinking about other things, and genuinely concentrate on and connect with your partner. Find something you can do together that you both like, whether it's a common interest, a dancing class, a regular stroll, or just sitting down for a cup of coffee in the morning.

- **Together, try something new.** Trying new activities as a group may be a great way to connect and keep things fresh. It might be as easy as trying a new restaurant or taking a day trip to a different location.Concentrate on having fun together. In the early phases of a relationship, couples are frequently more fun and lighthearted. This humorous approach, however, may often be lost when life obstacles arise or old resentments resurface. Having a sense of humor may help you get through difficult situations, decrease stress, and work through problems more readily. Consider creative methods to surprise your partner, such as bringing flowers home or suddenly scheduling a table at their favorite restaurant. Playing with dogs or young children may also help you rediscover your childlike side.

Participate in activities that assist others. One of the most effective strategies to remain close and connected is to concentrate on something outside of the relationship that both you and your partner appreciate. Volunteering for a cause, initiative, or community service that is meaningful to both of you may keep a relationship new and fresh. It may also introduce you to new people and ideas, create opportunities to solve new issues together, and provide new methods to engage with each other.

Doing activities to assist others provides enormous joy, in addition to relieving stress, worry, and sadness. Humans are hardwired to assist others. The more you help, the better you will feel as a person and as a couple.

- **Keep in touch through communication.**

A good relationship is built on effective communication. You feel comfortable and happy when you have a good emotional connection with your companion. When individuals stop speaking well, they stop interacting effectively, and times of transition or stress may exacerbate the distance. It may seem basic, but as long as you communicate, you can typically work through any issues you're having.

Don't leave your partner guessing about what you need.It's not always simple to express your needs. For one thing, many of us do not devote enough time to considering what is really essential to us in a relationship. Even if you are aware of what you need, discussing it might make you feel vulnerable, embarrassed, or even ashamed. But consider it from your partner's perspective. It is a joy, not a burden, to provide comfort and understanding to someone you care about.If you've been together for some time, you could believe that your partner understands what you're thinking and what you need. Your partner, on the other hand, is not a mind reader. While your partner may have an inkling, it is much better to explain your requirements clearly to prevent any misunderstanding.Your partner may detect something, but it may not be what you need.

Furthermore, people evolve, and what you needed and desired five years ago may be completely different today. Instead of allowing resentment, confusion, or rage to fester when your partner constantly gets it wrong, make it a practice to tell them precisely what you need.

- **Keep an eye out for your partner's nonverbal cues.**

What we don't say conveys so much of our conversation. Eye contact, tone of voice, posture, and gestures such as leaning forward, crossing your arms, or holding someone's hand express much more than words.

When you can read your partner's nonverbal signs, or "body language," you'll be able to determine how they really feel and react appropriately. To make a relationship work, each individual must be aware of their own and their partner's nonverbal clues. Your partner's reactions may vary from yours. For example, one individual may regard a hug after a difficult day as a loving way of communication, whilst another may prefer to go for a stroll or sit and talk.

It's also critical that what you say matches your body language. If you say "I'm OK," yet clench your teeth and turn away, your body is plainly communicating that you are everything but "fine."

You feel loved and joyful when you get positive emotional signals from your mate, and your partner feels the same when you deliver favorable emotional cues. When you lose interest in your own or your partner's emotions, the connection between you suffers, and your capacity to communicate suffers, particularly during difficult situations.

- ## Be an attentive listener.

While our culture places a high importance on talking, learning to listen in a manner that makes another person feel appreciated and understood may help you form a deeper, stronger bond.There is a significant distinction between this kind of listening and merely hearing. When you really listen—when you're engaged with what's being said—you'll notice small intonations in your partner's voice that reveal how they're truly feeling and the emotions they're attempting to transmit. Being a good listener does not obligate you to agree or alter your views. However, it will assist you in identifying shared points of view that might aid in dispute resolution.

- ## Control your tension.

When you're anxious or emotionally overloaded, you're more prone to misinterpret your romantic partner, give ambiguous or off-putting nonverbal cues, or fall into dangerous knee-jerk behavior patterns. How often have you been frustrated and yelled at a loved one, saying or doing something you afterwards regretted?

You will not only prevent such regrets if you can learn to rapidly handle tension and return to a calm condition, but you will also help to avoid disagreements and misunderstandings—and even help to calm your partner when tempers flare.

- **Maintain physical closeness.**

Touch is an essential component of human life. Infant brain development studies have revealed the value of frequent, loving interaction. And the advantages do not stop there. Affectionate touch raises oxytocin levels in the body, a hormone that impacts bonding and attachment.

While sex is frequently the foundation of a committed relationship, it should not be the primary form of physical closeness. Touch that is frequent and affectionate—holding hands, embracing, kissing—is also essential.

Of course, it's important to be aware of your partner's preferences. Unwanted touching or improper approaches might cause the other person to stiffen up and withdraw, which is the opposite of what you desire. As with so many other facets of a successful relationship, how effectively you express your wants and intentions to your partner may be crucial.

Even if you have a demanding job or small children, you can help to maintain physical closeness by scheduling regular couple time, whether it's a date night or just an hour at the end of the day when you can sit and speak or hold hands.

- **In your relationship, learn to give and take.**

If you expect to obtain what you want in a relationship 100% of the time, you will be disappointed. Compromise is the foundation of healthy partnerships.However, it requires effort on the part of each individual to ensure a fair transaction.

Recognize your partner's priorities.Understanding what is actually important to your partner may go a long way toward fostering goodwill and a climate of compromise. On the other hand, it is critical that your partner recognizes your desires and that you express them clearly. Giving constantly to others at the cost of your own needs can only lead to resentment and hostility.

**Make "winning" your objective.**

It will be difficult to find a compromise if you approach your partner with the mindset that things must be done your way or else.

This attitude might result from not having your needs addressed when you were younger, or it can be the result of years of collected animosity in the relationship reaching a boiling point. It's OK to be passionate about something, but your partner needs to be heard as well. Respect the other person and their point of view.

- **Learn how to handle disagreements in a courteous manner.**

Conflict is unavoidable in every relationship, but in order to maintain a healthy relationship, both individuals must feel heard. The aim is to maintain and deepen the connection, not to win.

Make certain that you are battling fairly. Maintain your concentration on the problem at hand while still respecting the other person. Don't get into fights about things that can't be altered.

Instead of explicitly attacking someone, use "I" phrases to express how you feel. Instead of stating, "You make me feel horrible," say, "I feel bad when you do that."

- **Don't bring up old disputes again**.

Rather than focusing on previous fights or grudges and assigning blame, consider what you can do today to remedy the situation.

- **Be ready to forgive**.

It is hard to resolve a disagreement if you are unwilling or unable to forgive others.

Take a break if tempers flare. Take a few minutes to relax and cool yourself before saying or doing anything you'll come to regret. Remember that you're fighting with someone you care about.

Understand when to let things go. If you can't agree on anything, at least agree to disagree. A dispute requires two participants to continue. If a disagreement isn't progressing, you might opt to disengage and move on.

- **Be prepared for ups and downs.**

It's important to remember that every relationship has ups and downs. You will not always be on the same wavelength. Sometimes one partner is dealing with a stressful circumstance, such as the loss of a close family member. Other situations, such as job loss or serious health difficulties, may have an impact on both couples and make it harder to connect with one another. You may have different views about how to manage your money or raise your children.

Various individuals deal with stress in different ways, and misunderstandings may quickly escalate into annoyance and fury.

Don't blame your partner for your difficulties. Life's difficulties sometimes cause us to lose our cool. When you are under a lot of stress, it may seem simpler to vent to your partner, and it may even seem safer to snap at them. Fighting like this may seem like a release at first, but it progressively ruins your relationship. Find better methods to deal with stress, rage, and irritation.

Trying to impose a solution might lead to even more issues. Everyone approaches difficulties and situations in their own unique manner. Remember that you are a group. Moving ahead together might help you get over the hard periods.

Consider the early phases of your relationship. Discuss the events that brought the two of you together, the point at which you started to drift apart, and how you might work together to recapture the feeling of falling in love. Be open to new experiences. Change is unavoidable in life, and you may either embrace it or oppose it. Flexibility is vital for adapting to the constant change that occurs in every relationship, and it helps you develop together through both the good and difficult times.

Reach out to outside aid for your relationship as a group. Problems in a relationship might often seem too complicated or overwhelming for you to manage as a pair. Couples counseling or chatting with a trustworthy friend or religious figure might be beneficial.

# Chapter 3

## <u>Sign that show someone love you</u>

Love isn't always perfect. In real life, things are often surprising, annoying, and even painful.

While it may undoubtedly provide several advantages, these benefits seldom arrive without some devoted work and a willingness to endure certain hardships as part of the process.

When you love someone, you choose to nourish the earliest stirrings of attraction, nourishing those early sentiments and fortifying them to withstand future challenges.

The task may not always seem to be simple. Nonetheless, many individuals consider the result — reciprocal, lifelong love — to be well worth the cost.

People often claim that you will know when someone loves you. There is some truth to it,

but it may not manifest itself in the lavish gestures shown in the media.
These symptoms generally indicate genuine affection.

- **You feel protected around them.**

The foundation of loving partnerships is safety. A loving companion will not physically harm you or ruin your property. They will also not intimidate or coerce you into doing things you don't want to do, make choices for you, or isolate you from social support.

Feeling secure also includes being able to make your own choices and express yourself without fear of being judged by others. When you communicate your thoughts and ambitions, you are met with support rather than dismissal or criticism.

- **They pay attention.**

A loving companion will be interested in the specifics of your life.Instead of instantly turning the discussion to their own experiences, they will actively listen by asking questions and waiting their turn to contribute. Instead of being dismissed with a distracted "Uh yeah" or "Wow, that stinks," you get the impression they really care.

While they may not hear or remember everything you say, they will have a good idea of what is important to you: your likes and dislikes, hopes and anxieties, friendships and family connections, and so on.

Partners in a healthy relationship accept both the good and the negative. When you bring up worries or relationship issues, they will consider your emotions rather than disregard or minimize your discomfort.

- **They accept your peculiarities rather than attempt to alter you.**

You and your partner are distinct individuals, so you won't feel the same way about everything, no matter how much you share.Someone who cares about you will embrace your unique thoughts and emotions as part of who you are. They may engage in some polite debate, but they will show an interest in your point of view rather than pushing you to accept theirs.When requested, a loving partner may provide counsel and advice, but they will not attempt to restrict your decisions or conduct. They will also refrain from showing love or criticizing you until you agree with them.

In general, you'll feel more at ease when you agree to disagree.Everyone feels irritated and angry at times, but there are healthy methods to vent rage. A loving partner will not threaten you, use anger to punish you, or make you afraid.

If they do have an angry outburst, they may agree to get therapy immediately — not just to better themselves but also because they observed your anxiety and want to make you feel secure again.

- **You can easily converse.**

Love requires open and honest communication. This does not imply that you must share every notion you have. Everyone has private sentiments, and it's perfectly OK to keep them to yourself.Over the course of your relationship, your partner will most likely do something that irritates you, whether it's snoring or being so engrossed in a TV program that they forget to pick you up from work.

Instead of picking at every tiny aggravation, you may find it more useful to vent to a buddy about these little irritations.Still, you can't read each other's thoughts, so if you want your relationship to grow, you need to speak about the topics that actually matter. A loving partner will recognize the desire to communicate and will be there, both physically and mentally, when the time comes for a dialogue.Good communication may include:

- Disclosing feelings
- Identifying and addressing conflict zones
- establishing a connection via physical or emotional closeness.
- Confirming connection boundaries
- Detecting messages through body language

Everyone struggles with communication. Rather than believing that a partner who struggles to explain ideas and feelings does not love you, consider their desire to acquire and practice stronger communication skills.

- **They urge you to pursue your own interests.**

Partners should, without a doubt, appreciate one another's presence. A loving partner, on the other hand, will understand your unique personality outside of the relationship and will support you when you want to spend time with friends or pursue your own interests. They'll also keep their own connections and hobbies rather than relying on you to amuse or meet all of their social demands.

Your partner may disagree with how you spend your time. When you do something that bothers them, such as spending a lot of time with a toxic buddy or drinking excessively, they may express polite concern: "I've observed [X] isn't always very pleasant to you," for example.They may also establish limits for themselves, such as "I don't want to hang out with you while you're intoxicated." They will not, however, attempt to restrict your friends, your choices, or your conduct.

- **You have mutual trust.**

Trust generally grows with love, and you won't usually find one without the other. A loving partner will most likely trust you until you betray them. They will not ask you if you see your friends, are followed, or use your phone or computer.If they have no cause to suspect you of deception, they will not accuse you of lying or cheating, nor will they demand you travel everywhere together.

Trust also implies that people feel comfortable enough to express their thoughts and feelings, speak up about their problems, and seek assistance.If you mislead, cheat, or betray them, this trust may be broken. Because love frequently persists when trust has been destroyed, it is possible to reestablish trust – but only with time, honesty, and hard effort.

- **They make an attempt.**

While attraction may come in an instant, true love takes more time and effort.It may seem romantic if someone determines you're "meant to be" or says "I think I love you" after just one day. However, this might indicate a domineering or manipulative nature rather than a sincere romance. With so many individuals on the planet, the concept of one-and-only instant love may seem weak. Sure, soul mates may exist, but it's crucial to remember that love seldom happens overnight.

Someone who really cares will strive to develop your love from the ground up and reinforce it at every turn by:

- Putting family time first
- I'm expressing an interest in getting to know you.

- being willing to discuss differences or conflicts.
- deciding to experiment with new things jointly
- committing themselves as partners to mutual growth.

- **You are aware of your ability to cooperate or compromise.**

Conflict does not inherently make a relationship dysfunctional, but how you manage it does. A "my way or the highway" attitude does not imply a caring relationship. Someone who loves you will not look at you with disdain, will not insist on being right, and will not listen to you.

In healthy relationships, both parties collaborate to discover solutions to problems such as communication or intimacy. You may make certain sacrifices for the sake of your relationship, but you should not be the only one.A partner who loves you will make personal sacrifices to discover a solution that will satisfy both of you.Maybe neither of you got all you wanted, yet meeting in the center might make you both happy.

- **They assist you in meeting your requirements.**

While no one individual can fulfill all of your requirements, romantic relationships may provide significant emotional support. Many individuals desire romantic relationships precisely for this reason.A loving partner cannot (and should not) do everything for you, but they will rejoice in your victories and be there for you when you fall.They'll help when they can and provide ideas or useful recommendations when they can't.If they are unable to assist you, such as with mental health problems, severe financial stress, or a workplace difficulty, they will recommend that you seek appropriate aid.You can always depend on them to be kind and to listen.

- **They admire you.**

Respect is essential for the survival of loving partnerships.

A partner that respects you will demonstrate their appreciation for you and your time together. They will also support your decisions, even if they do not agree with them.

Other respectable behaviors to look for include:

- honesty
- Communication is clear and timely.
- Even during fights, courteous and thoughtful language
- There is no need to push your limits.


- **Every day, you see it:**

Perhaps your companion does not bring you lunch at work or lavish you with expensive presents.

But once you go to the kitchen, they always give you a cup of coffee. They never forget your dates, and they always grin when you enter the room.

Love is most obvious in the mundane details of daily life. Someone who loves you may just be a consistent, loving presence in your life rather than sweep you off your feet with costly gestures.They turn up for both the good and the bad, demonstrating that you can bank on their continuing support. These subtler demonstrations of devotion may not excite you as much as a public rendition of your favorite love song, but they are sure to linger long after the final notes of the music have died away.

- **They want what is best for you.**

Forever together may not automatically imply "love." When love is still there, it's generally feasible to save a failing relationship, but irreconcilable differences may mean you're better off moving on to find someone who's a better match. Assume one of you wants children and the other does not. Or maybe you've always wanted to live on the East Coast near your family, yet they can't imagine living anywhere else in the Pacific Northwest. When it is evident that your relationship has run its course, someone who genuinely loves you will let you go.

Love isn't all or nothing, and passionate love may evolve into an enduring friendship over time. Even if you can't keep a friendship going, it's never a bad idea to treasure that residual favorable respect.

In conclusion,

A caring partner will share your desire to develop together and build your relationship.

Relationship skills, on the other hand, may not come naturally to everyone, and some individuals need additional assistance in learning how to communicate emotions in healthy ways. Couples therapy may be a wonderful place to explore this together.

# Chapter 4

# **How to resolve conflict with your partner**

It's easy to overlook one thing in today's world of dating reality programs, smartphone applications, and romantic comedies: partnerships involve labor. We seldom "swipe right," fall in love, and then live happily ever after. When things become rough, it's easy to give up, claim "it wouldn't have worked out anyway," and move on - rather than putting in the effort to learn how to overcome disagreement in a relationship.

Disagreements in partnerships occur for a variety of reasons, ranging from basic daily disagreements such as who does the dishes to significant ones such as adultery. Lack of attraction and desire, emotional stonewalling and loss of commitment, as well as economics, family duties, and uncertainty, are all frequent relationship difficulties. Stress in other parts of our life has an affect on our relationships as well: When you return home from work dissatisfied and fatigued, or when you're arguing with other friends or family members, your stress spreads. To enhance your relationship, you must learn how to settle disagreement in all aspects of your life.

## 1. INSPECT YOUR FOCUS

The focus defines the direction. If your goal is to create a beautiful, passionate relationship, you will succeed.

When you are focused on protecting yourself from an attack rather than tackling the issue, disagreements in relationships become detrimental. By concentrating on your pain and suffering, you ensure that you will experience more of the same, since energy flows where concentration goes. "Whatever we continually concentrate on is precisely what we will experience in our life,"

Jack used to drive along a two-lane roadway with just power line poles every 10-20 yards. One of these seems to be always adorned with flowers, candles, and photos. With so much room on each side of the post, it was incredible how many people had died or been wounded after colliding with it. Why didn't the victim run away? Why didn't they veer to one side or the other?

It's because folks would be so focused on avoiding striking the pole. Our emphasis, however, defines our course. If we don't want to strike the pole, we must concentrate on what we do want: to remain on the road! We may affect the outcome by shifting our emphasis.

This lesson is about how to save a relationship. If you concentrate on where you don't want your relationship to go, arguing and allowing resentment to fester, you'll wind up where you don't want to be - either in a miserable, unfulfilling relationship or split from your partner entirely. If you concentrate on resolving disagreement and developing together, you will get the desired results.

## 2. TALK TO OTHERS

You are now seated in a coffee shop. There are two couples seated close to you in the store. The couple to your left is debating whether or not to go out to supper with friends. "It's never enjoyable, as you stated last time," he adds. "Of course you would say that, because they're my pals, and you've never given any of my friends a chance," she answers. He rolls his eyes and adds, sarcastically, "Here we go." War and Peace, our particular copy, whatever volume." They sat in silence, turning away from one other.

The pair to your right is similarly debating whether to go out to supper with their buddies. "I think I'm a bit scared that it'll go on for hours and that it may not be very pleasant," he admits. "What are your thoughts?" "I understand," she says. I really want to attend, but as a compromise, maybe we can set a time when we have to leave?" "Besides, it'll be nice to get home early," she says, touching his hand and smiling. He nods and smiles as they continue to read and drink coffee.

Both couples faced a dilemma - the identical one, in fact. However, one understood how to handle disagreement in a relationship while the other did not. One responded by depending on negative habits, and the dispute served to deepen the chasm between them. The other person utilized the disagreement to express their emotions and strengthen their bond. Which pair do you believe has the most successful and satisfying relationship? Which relationship do you believe will continue the longest? Communication is critical for resolving conflicts in relationships.

## 3. MAKE CONFLICT AN OPPORTUNITY

One couple at the coffee shop found how to handle disputes in a relationship: don't see it as a competition. Why would you want to lose your lover, the person you care about? When you recognize that there are no losers in love, you can let go of little disagreements and embrace good communication.

Conflicts provide chances for you and your partner to align on values and results. They provide opportunities to comprehend, accept, and embrace diversity. Put yourself in your partner's shoes and try to comprehend their situation. These events and feelings may be unpleasant, but if we constantly choose comfort, we will never develop.

Conflict may also help you discover more about your relationship and love them in a deeper way. Learn to perceive disputes as opportunities to go forward rather than causes to retreat. When you disagree with your partner and are wondering how to salvage your relationship, choose to recognize the best in the circumstance and actively opt to work toward a more solid future together.

## 4. MAKE USE OF HUMOR

If you find yourself in a retaliatory spiral, a helpful strategy is to disrupt the cycle with comedy. Humor may help you and your partner concentrate on what you both want - learning how to salvage your relationship - rather than what you both don't want - another fruitless dispute. If you see an argument building, take a step back and derail it. Argue as though you were Christopher Walken or William Shatner. Sing a funny song to your partner. Make the dispute absurd.

Let us return to the coffee shop example to demonstrate this concept. You see an elderly couple. The guy spills his tea all over the table, including some of his wife's favorite clothing. He gets up to fetch some napkins, and she laughs and quips to the other diners, "He's been doing this to me for 20 years - never completed a cup yet!" He returns, dabs the tea off her, and tells the other customers, "She asked for it!" They both laugh, as do you and everyone else in the store.

Some couples might have turned the scenario into a fight, but by utilizing comedy to halt the retaliatory spiral, this husband and wife grasp the chance to learn how to overcome conflict in a relationship.

5. ASK APPROPRIATE QUESTIONS

If you're wondering how to preserve your relationship, it's likely that things have been going bad for a while. To find the true, deeper concerns, you must not only turn to the past, but also to the future. It all comes down to asking yourself the correct questions.

First, make sure you're approaching this practice with the appropriate mentality. The aim is not to assign blame, rehash prior disputes, or list all the things your partner does that irritate you. You must shift your perspective to one of thankfulness and acceptance. Accept that life is occurring to you, not to you. Even the current situation of your relationship is an opportunity to learn and develop if you are willing to listen to what it has to say.

You are now ready to ask yourself important questions: Why did your relationship fail? What are the limiting ideas that you and your partner have had that have harmed your relationship? How will you get over them? And what do you want to achieve in the future? What will be the focal point of your relationship?

## 6. ACCEPTANCE OF PRACTICE

Apply your new abundant perspective to your relationship. Because no human being is flawless, all of our partners have annoying tendencies. Instead of focusing on their flaws, consider what they bring to the table, how they make you feel, and the characteristics you like. You'll quickly realize that even the things that used to irritate you are now part of that full person, your partner, whom you cherish.

Do you remember the two couples from the café? The successful couple confirmed their support for one another by putting effort into understanding each other's needs - she supported his need to depart at a specific hour, and he supported her desire to interact with friends. Instead of allowing something trivial to escalate into a large conflict, they spoke with one another, evaluated one another's needs, and made it a pleasant problem to solve.Listen to your partner, comprehend what they are saying, and comprehend why they feel the way they do. Accept yourself as well: be honest about your own feelings and emotions. Be true to yourself. You're not wondering how to repair your relationship because of personal shortcomings. They're really a wonderful instrument for expressing your affection for your mate.

## 7. BE CONSCIOUS OF YOUR NEGATIVE PATTERNS

Humans are habitual animals. We all have patterns that influence our choices and actions, both good and bad. We may react defensively to our relationships or withdraw inside and blame ourselves for marital difficulties, shutting down but ultimately erupting. Many of us fall back on old tricks like giving our relationships space or even the quiet treatment.Whether you were asked if you knew how to settle disagreements, you'd pretty likely answer yes; if they asked if the silent treatment or ignoring the matter were wise methods to deal with conflict, you'd almost certainly say no. You should know better than to stoop to such ridiculous measures, but if you're in enough pain, you do it anyway. Why? Why fall back on negative behaviors instead of striving to address the underlying communication issues?

## 8. PRACTICE FORGIVENESS

You're probably furious, resentful, wounded, mistrustful, and a slew of other unpleasant feelings if you're asking how to salvage your relationship since your trust was destroyed. If you were the one who betrayed the trust, you probably feel terrible and humiliated. You could even attempt to blame or defend your behavior. In this case, both parties must work on forgiveness.

You won't instantly become forgiving toward your lover one day. Forgiveness is an ongoing process. It's a series of modest actions that pile up over time, such as acknowledging errors, practicing absolute honesty, and putting your partner first. It takes effort to forgive.

If you were the one who violated the trust, you must accept full responsibility. Respect your partner's feelings and offer them the space they need. Put your relationship first, and avoid the cycle of self-blame. If your trust has been damaged, give yourself some space while continuing to communicate. Tell your partner what you need to do to reestablish trust. Above all, never give up.

## 9. ALLOW TIME FOR TOUCH

When you're always arguing with your partner, when everything they do irritates you, it's difficult to remain loving. You must, however, make time for touch. This includes snuggling on the sofa watching a movie, stealing a morning embrace before work, and holding hands for no purpose at all.

There's a reason why hugging your mate feels so good: Cuddling, embracing, and simply holding hands causes the brain to generate oxytocin, a "feel-good" molecule that makes you feel secure and loved. Oxytocin may help you sleep better, feel more connected to your mate, and even reduce your blood pressure. All of these advantages are yours just by reaching across and grasping your partner's hand.If you withhold physical love, even if you're angry, you can end yourself in a sexless marriage. Start with physical contact if you really want to resolve a relationship dispute. Cuddle before going to bed. When you're out to supper with pals, hold hands. Sneak a kiss while you're preparing supper. Physical affection does not occur as a byproduct of a good relationship; rather, it is the cause of a happy relationship.

Relationships are difficult. We're all human, and we all make errors. We all have shortcomings. Sometimes we just don't put in the necessary effort, and our relationships suffer as a result. When we begin to investigate how to manage conflict in a relationship, it may have been ignored for years. But keep in mind that many relationships are worth preserving. You just must be willing to put in the effort.

# Chapter 5

## **Behavior to keep your partner**

People frequently rush into a relationship without having clarity about what they want and what the other is expecting. If you want to be in a fulfilling relationship, you may want to know the fundamental relationship conduct. Unfortunately, most relationships break apart after the first enthusiasm and bring misery to the couple. A partnership without a vision will lead you nowhere.

### 1. Love without any conditions:

Love cannot have conditions.It gets all too materialistic when "only ifs" permeate into your relationship. You cannot limit your love if your spouse earns more than you, gives you gifts every month, and always looks beautiful.Love your partner unconditionally, just as your parents love you.

2. Make your relationship your top priority.

Make your relationship your top priority. Invest time and effort in your relationship and continually attempt to make it better.

3.Keep a line of communication open:

Without communication, your relationship may deteriorate.Let your conversation be open and honest. No matter how busy or weary you are, don't allow it to hinder your communication.

4. Hug as often as possible:

Make it a daily habit to make your hugs last longer.Hugging boosts oxytocin (the love hormone) levels and lowers cortisol ( the stress hormone) (1). (1).

5. Have sex generously: Don't arrange sex, let it be spontaneous. That's when it gets thrilling and the connection between you deepens. Don't allow any excuses to get in your way when it comes to having sex.

6. Plan a date night to spend quality time together.

You may even have a romantic supper at home. Simply relax in the garden or balcony and replay your memories or watch your favorite TV show together. The aim is to take a break from your hectic schedules to remain close.

7.Be honest and truthful to build trust.

Honesty and truthfulness are the foundations of trust. Occasional little and harmless lies are tolerated to make your spouse pleased, but infidelity has no place in a relationship.

8. Critique but don't hurt:

If you want to criticize your spouse to make them better, then the criticism should be constructive and positive. Help your spouse realize the purpose behind the criticism.

9. Have a healthy argument:

Arguing is healthy as long as it is not frequent and harmful. You may agree to disagree amicably. Make it a practice of listening intently and arguing less. That displays your regard for each other.

10. Stick by each other:

We wish bad times did not affect your life, but it's at these moments you have to stand by your spouse and display your unshakeable love for each other. That's when your connection strengthens.

11. Recognize and thank your partner for everything, no matter how simple or mundane the task.It demonstrates that you respect and appreciate them, both of which are vital for a long-lasting relationship.

12. Take and give some personal space.

Being close to your spouse does not imply growing attached to them. Give them their own space, leave them alone for a day, and let them relax the way they choose. Similarly, make sure you are receiving your share of me-time to pursue your profession, interests, or simply relax.

13. Celebrate the big days:

Do not forget the crucial days in your relationship-the day you first met each other, your first date, the day your spouse proposed to you, and, of course, your birthdays and wedding anniversary. Celebrate your bonding and create memorable moments.

## 14. Understand and sympathize with your partner:

If your partner is having a bad day and screams at you, resist the urge to respond in kind. They might have had a bad day at work or be stressed out. At first, sympathize with them, and when the moment is suitable, find out what is upsetting them.

## 15.Be willing to forgive and forget.

Mistakes happen. If your lover hurts you, forgive him/her and forget about it. It will inspire them to do the same when you make a mistake.

## 16. Show interest in your spouse's hobbies or activities:

Does your partner pursue a sport that you find boring? You don't have to tell them that! Instead, attempt to understand the sport and question your spouse about it. Show interest and engage in your partner's hobbies. You will come to enjoy them.

## 17. Ask what you want:

Don't expect your spouse to comprehend all your requirements and wishes. Telepathy will not function all the time. If you need anything, simply ask for it.

## 18. Accept your flaws:

Nobody is perfect!Accept your partner as they are, flaws and all. Relationships are about being the proper partner, not the ideal partner, since perfect doesn't exist.

Keeping your promises makes you trustworthy and dependable, which boosts your reputation.

## 20. Do the best and be the best you can be.

All of us are subject to criticism and fear-the dread of doing something wrong and being condemned for it. Give your best to your relationship, irrespective of your partner's response. There is only so much you can do; the way your spouse responds to it is not in your control.

Behavior is not only about doing something correctly; it is also about avoiding doing certain things.

Things You Should Not Do In A Relationship:

Discuss your prior romances and exes.

Take your mate for granted.

Go to bed furious.

Strive to be the perfect companion.

Try to mend or modify the individual.

Discuss your difficulties with friends or relatives.

It can seem clichéd, but partnerships involve work, time, and love.

www.ingramcontent.com/pod-product-compliance
Lightning Source LLC
Chambersburg PA
CBHW060911130726
48001CB00006B/2187